Dana
Griepentrog

BAD MOM CARDS

COLLECT THE ENTIRE SET!

#4: ESTHER J.

Ran out of orange juice one morning and served kids orange soda instead.

#17: GLORIA B.

Promised to take daughter to the mall after school — and then didn't.

#20: JAYNE R.

Sent child to school with 99.1°F. temperature — and child was sent home.

#23: LUCY L.

And then he...

Told friend "funny" story about kid and had a laugh at kid's expense.

#35: MARTINA F.

EASTER
ST. PATRICK'S
XMAS
XMA

Didn't put up the St. Patrick's Day decorations one year.

#39: DAWN K.

When daughter left stuffed bear in Grand Union, waited until next day to retrieve it.

#48: SUZIE M.

Let kid play two hours of Nintendo — *just to get him out of her hair.*

#61: DEBORAH Z.

Has never even *tried* to make Play-Doh from scratch.

#89: BECKY O.

While on phone, told child to *SHUT THE HELL UP,* or she would brain her.

R. Chast

CHILDPROOF

CARTOONS BY
ROZ CHAST

HYPERION

NEW YORK

Several of these cartoons originally appeared in
The New Yorker (Copyright © 1987, 1988, 1989, 1990, 1991,
1992, 1993, 1994, 1995, 1996, 1997 by the New Yorker Magazine, Inc.)
Grateful acknowledgement is made to The New Yorker for
permission to reprint.

Other cartoons have appeared in The Sciences, Child, Worth,
Ladies Home Journal, Self, New Woman, and Allure.

Library of Congress Cataloging-in-Publication Data

Chast, Roz
    Childproof: cartoons about parents and children/Roz Chast —
1st ed.
      p. cm.
ISBN 0-7868-6244-0
1. Parents and children — Caricature and cartoons. 2. American
    wit and humor, Pictorial. I. Title
NC1429. C525A4 1997
741.5'973 — dc21

                                97-1081
                                CIP

FIRST EDITION
10 9 8 7 6 5 4 3 2 1

TO MY CHILDREN

TO MY PARENTS

Almost eleven years ago, I decided it was time I started doing something about becoming a mom, and amazingly, my husband went obligingly along with this not-fully-thought-out plan. At the time, we

fig. 1
In happier, less responsible days

were living in a stoveless studio apartment on the Upper West Side of Manhattan. We socialized. We went to the movies, plays, and the opera. We ate out a lot. We ordered in a lot. We worked on our projects. We hung around the apartment in our pajamas. We did not, on the spur of the moment, fly to Paris, go on a Land of the Midnight Sun cruise, bungee jump, or pal around with models. Nonetheless, we were having more fun than we were ever to have again in our entire lives. A friend who was already a parent told us: "Having children will turn your lives into a

living hell." He added darkly, "Don't do it." We thought he was joking. How naive we were.

Over the next few years, we put aside our own childish things to make room for all the new, fluorescent-hued childish things that were soon to arrive. In short, we started a family. First came our son. Our daughter followed a few years later. As they grew, I began to fully appreciate our friend's warning about how kids would transform our

fig. 2
Dog head

lives. We suddenly found ourselves living with people who kept going to pieces over stuff that you and I would consider trivial or simply bizarre. Something as innocuous as a half-inch by half-inch photo of a dog's head scissored out of a magazine ad could become the center of a nightmarish property battle that lasts for 36 hours, and

that even if you've read every parenting book on Earth (which I hope you haven't), you will still not be able to resolve. Your temptation to

fig. 3
A big mistake that
you will regret

coerce a boy into wearing a pale-blue-and-white striped shirt that brings out the color of his eyes will probably result in a lifetime of therapy for him. One day, when you are minding your own business, a teacher will telephone you at home to inform you that your child is tormenting her, and imply that it is *your fault*.

Fortunately for everybody, there are those other times, when you catch a glimpse of your kids absorbed in some egg-carton project or video game, and your heart contracts, and you realize that you would do anything to keep them safe and happy, because despite the supermarket tantrums, the homework fights, the family car trips that should never have taken place—they are still the center of your universe. Plus, the day will soon come when your kids' feet will be bigger than yours, and they will be shaving and doing other unpleasant, grown-up things. So you try to keep it all in perspective. And when all else fails, you can draw—or read—cartoons about it.

Roz Chast

January 2, 1997

Fifteen years of fertility treatments... hundreds of thousands of dollars... if you don't get into Harvard, I'll kill myself.

AMERICA'S TEN MOST WANTED
BABIES

Timmy:
Waking repeatedly
during night.

Lulu:
Throwing tantrum
in A & P.

Mark:
Hurling trayful of
creamed spinach on
floor.

Missy:
Cajoling adult into
purchase of $40.⁰⁰ toys,
then ignoring it.

Donald:
Eating cat's
food.

Lon:
Putting banana
into VCR.

Jeanette:
Licking car
tire.

Shelley:
Refusing to kiss
Grandma.

Susie:
Biting other
baby in
playground.

Wilbur:
Giving up
morning nap.

R. Chast

NEW ITEMS FROM

FIRST CHILD, CATALOGUE

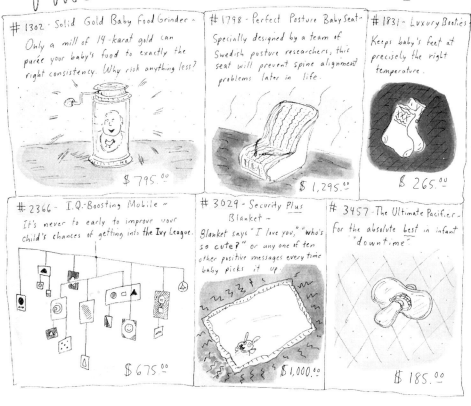

#1302 - Solid Gold Baby Food Grinder -
Only a mill of 14-karat gold can purée your baby's food to exactly the right consistency. Why risk anything less?

$795.⁰⁰

#1798 - Perfect Posture Baby Seat -
Specially designed by a team of Swedish posture researchers, this seat will prevent spine alignment problems later in life.

$1,295.⁰⁰

#1831 - Luxury Booties -
Keeps baby's feet at precisely the right temperature.

$265.⁰⁰

#2366 - I.Q.-Boosting Mobile ~
It's never to early to improve your child's chances of getting into the Ivy League.

$675.⁰⁰

#3029 - Security Plus Blanket ~
Blanket says "I love you," "who's so cute?" or any one of ten other positive messages every time baby picks it up.

$1,000.⁰⁰

#3457 - The Ultimate Pacifier -
For the absolute best in infant "downtime".

$185.⁰⁰

R.Ch

SUCCESSFUL CHILDING

Be as bouncy, tiny, and cute as you possibly can.

Remember to be completely dependent.

Cry whenever you damn well feel like it.

R. Chast

NEW SELECTIONS

FROM THE

OUT LIKE A LIGHT ®

BOOK CLUB

NO BOOK LONGER THAN ONE PAGE IN OUR ENTIRE STOCK!

#329

#401

#457

R. Chast

MOMS

OVERLY INTERACTIVE TV

GIFTS FOR MOM

Beautiful Earrings

Go ahead, buy them. She'll exclaim over them and you'll never see them again.

Great Blouse

Unfortunately, it's not quite her style, her size, or her color.

Scarf

It's so nice! In fact, it's too nice.

Pretty Wine Glasses

One day when you're visiting her, she'll say, "Would you like these back? I never use them."

Desk Calendar for 1997

By the time you read this, it'll be winging its way to Aunt Edina.

BUTTERFLIES OF THE WORLD

1997

THE 41 ELM DRIVE BUGLE

★★★ MAY 15, 1992 EVENING EDITION
THE NEWSPAPER SPECIFICALLY FOR THE PERSON WHO GOES OFF TO WORK

BABY SITTER NEVER ARRIVES, NEVER CALLS!!!

HOUSE IN COMPLETE CHAOS

CON'T. PAGE 2

MOM SHOPS FOR GROCERIES

PICKS WRONG CHECKOUT LINE

TOT THROWS TANTRUM, STRANGERS STARE

SINK IN UPSTAIRS BATHROOM SLOW

NO CAUSE FOUND

CON'T. PAGE 5

CAT TEARS DEN CURTAIN

CON'T. PAGE 6

CON'T. PAGE 11

IN EVERY ISSUE:

HEIMLICH'S MOTHER'S MANEUVERS

The Skinned-Knee Maneuver -

Go on and on about person's bravery. Then place the hugest Band-Aid you can find over the icky area.

What a BIG BOY you are!

The Anti-Nausea Maneuver ~

Cajole person into eating a small piece of plain chicken and sipping some warm, flat ginger ale.

Have just a little.

The Splinter-Removal Maneuver ~

Have person look at the ceiling and think happy thoughts while you dig around with a needle.

R. Cht

UPCOMING ARTICLES IN

GUILT
MAGAZINE

1,001 Ways to Decorate
Your Child's Lunchbox

Complete Outfits to Make
For Each and Every One of
Your Kid's Dolls, Including
Shoes and Hats

Build Your Little One A
Model Railroad From Scratch

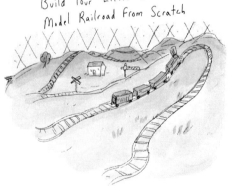

You Can Bake An Entire Farm—
Barn, Silo, and Lots of Animals
Out of Cookie Dough

R. Chast

DAYUS HORRIBILUS

Come... let us journey to

THE LAND OF THE
UNCOMFORTABLE PAUSE

~ THIS WEEK: AT THE PARK ~

~ NEXT WEEK: AN ENCOUNTER IN A SUPERMARKET ~

R. Chast

GOOFUS'S MOM

Leaves Goofus in the den with video games and six candy bars so she can go upstairs and read a novel.

GALLANT'S MOM

Takes Gallant to swimming lesson. Stops by a museum on the way home. Before lunch, they work on his science project together. Then she makes him a healthful sandwich on bread she baked the night before.

r.cw

BAD MOM. CARDS:

SPECIAL HOLIDAY EDITION

#137 - JAYNE L.~ Refused to even _attempt_ to make a gingerbread house.

#209 ~ EVELYN S.~ Fed entire family turkey TV dinners at Thanksgiving.

#311 ~ BETTY ANN K.~ Tried to convince everyone to skip presents this year.

#387 ~ DARLA A.~ Has never, _ever_ taken kids to the mall to see Santa.

#552 ~ CAROL P.~ Thinks Christmas lights and roof reindeer are a "fire hazard."

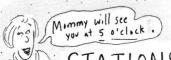

STATIONS ALONG THE
MOMMY TRACK

INTRODUCING...

Healing Truths

MOTHER'S DAY CARDS

To Mother

ON THIS VERY
SPECIAL DAY

→

You knew I wanted Barbie,
The world's most perfect teen.
Instead, you chose to buy me
A generic figurine.

Thanks for saving three dollars.

TO A DEAR PERSON

On Mother's Day

→

You did the best with the skills you had.
Considering everything, you weren't so bad.

I'll try not to repeat your mistakes.

WITH GOOD
WISHES ON
THIS DAY

TO MOM

→

Your house is always clean and neat,
Your lemon poundcake can't be beat.
Self-negating mom and wife,
It's not too late to get a life.

Only trying to help.

R. Chast

DISCIPLINE

THE MANY FACES OF NO

PARENTING WONKS

SHOPPING TRIP
OF THE DAMNED

Discovering
The Child Within

THE DIALOGUES OF PLATO

Phrieda: Plato, what do you want for lunch?

Plato: Anything. Whatever.

Phrieda: How's tuna?

Plato: Not tuna.

Phrieda: I could make you some scrambled eggs.

Plato: Grilled cheese.

Phrieda: We don't have any cheese.

Plato: I want grilled cheese!

Phrieda: I'll go to the store later and buy some cheese, but right now we don't have any cheese, so tell me: what do you want for lunch?

Plato: I don't want anything.

Phrieda: You have to have something.

Plato: You can't force me.

NEW LISTINGS

Camp Get-Out-of-My-Hair-for-Two-Weeks

The little ones will have the time of their lives while you and your spouse try to remember why you married each other.

Camp I'll-Miss-You-Now-Go

Picture your kid in a safe, bucolic environment, and you, doing the Sunday crossword uninterrupted.

Camp See-You-Later

Jimmy or Janie will enjoy a fun-filled summer. Meanwhile, you can go to Europe.

Camp Skedaddle

The apple of your eye can hike, swim, ride horseback, canoe, do arts and crafts, and make new friends. And you? You don't have to do a damn thing.

SINGIN' IN THE RAIN

THE SOUNDS OF SILENCE

ON THE ROAD TO RUIN

Parents said it was okay to drop violin lessons.

"If you're sure that's what you want to do!"

No computer in household.

"We're just about to buy one."

"We're *on the* verge."

Stayed up til one A.M. to watch "Goldfinger" on a school night.

"So what! It's a classic."

Was not informed of the seriousness of the pre-school interview.

"Just HAVE FUN!"

"No matter what happens, we'll still love you!"

THE NATIONAL PARTY GAMES ADVISORY BOARD'S REVISED "SIMON SAYS" TECHNIQUE

THE HEART OF DARKNESS

THE CAST OF CHARACTERS:

Baby Lucy

Mommy

Child's Tape Recorder/ Cassette Player

One afternoon...

HONEY! Don't chew on that!!!

BITE BITE BITE BITE

Why?

Because you might get electro-cuted.

And all my bones would show? Like a skeleton?

Not exactly.

You have nothing to worry about unless the tape recorder falls into the bath-tub with you.

What if I THROW it in?

Well, as long as you're not in the water, you CAN'T GET ELECTROCUTED.

But don't "throw it in."

PLEASE, GOD, LET SOMETHING HAPPEN TO END THIS CONVERSATION.

WHOOPS!

R-R-RING!!

I've got to answer the phone!

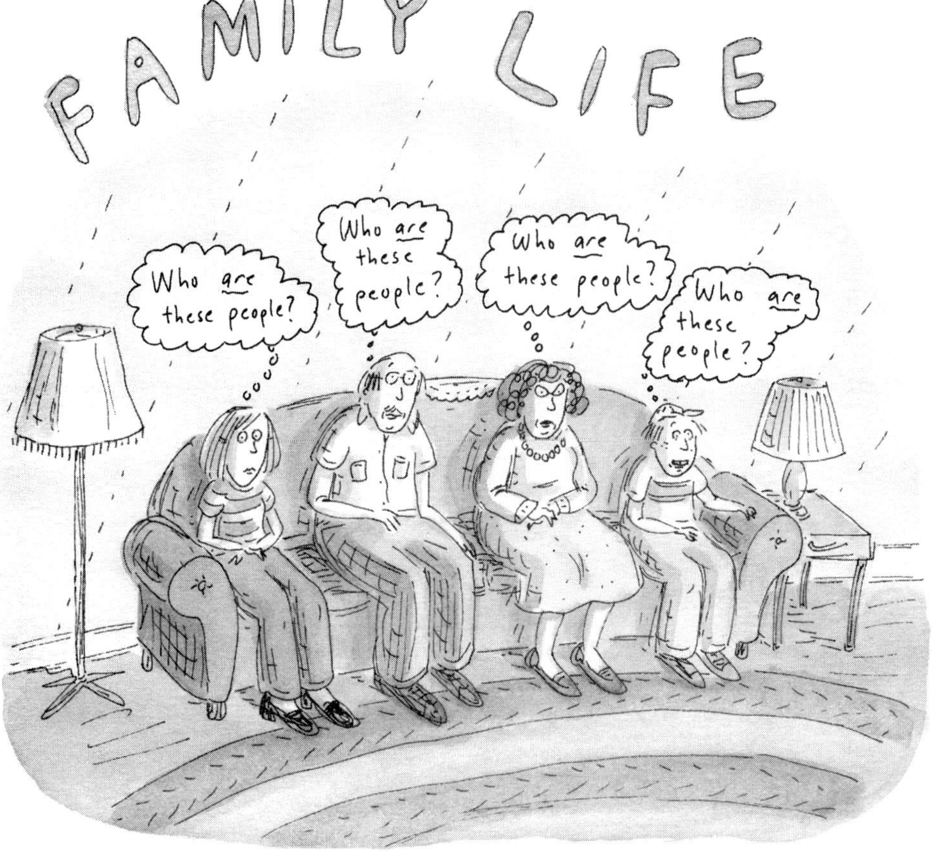

Little Lord Munchausen

CHILDREN OF
CELEBRITY CANINES

BRITTANY:
Daughter of Lassie. Hopes to become an actress/model. Not completely without talent, but close.

LANCE:
Benji's offspring. At the moment, wants to be a rock-and-roll drummer. A borderline socio-pathic ne'er-do-well.

SO WHATCHA LOOKIN' AT, HUH?

ROVER:
Son of Andalusian Dog. Happy and well adjusted. Nothing at all like his dad.

R. Chast

SINCE YOU ASKED

Ingredients: snips, snails, snail by-products, puppy-dog tails, other puppy-dog by-products.

Ingredients: sugar, aspartame, spice, everything nice, a blend of nutritive and non-nutritive sweeteners.

HOME ECONOMICS

LAY-Z-FAMILY© RECLINER

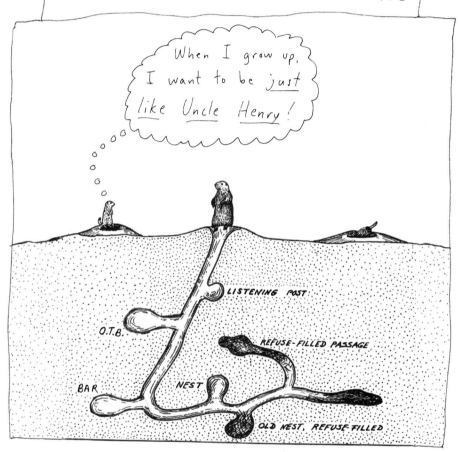

Prairie Dog Burrow.

FALLOUT

THE ALL-TEMP FAMILY
I'm only here til Thursday.
I leave on Friday.
I'll be here til mid-April.

NEW TITLES

FROM THE "PLUS KIDS" SERIES

R. Chast

CHILDREN'S PERSONALS

NEW IN NBRHD –
Just moved in. Girl, 9, wishes to meet other girls, 8-10. Likes Barbie, Ken, Skipper. Box 101.

BOY W/ICKY PARENTS–
I need a rebellious peer group, ages 10-12. Serious replies only. Box 215.

GIRL, 4, LOOKING FOR IMGNRY FRIEND–
Humans need not apply. Photo a must. Box 643.

R. Chast

Metamorphosis II

One day, Gregor Samsa awoke and found himself transformed into a caterpillar.

His family was quite upset, and at first, they were pretty ticked off at him about it.

You're so self-centered.

This is going to cost us a fortune.

The whole thing is SO EMBARRASSING.

Eventually, they got used to him, and life settled back into a comfortable routine.

Did you feed Gregor?

Yes, Mom.

I got him a new toy he might like.

If only it had all ended there.

MOM! DAD! GREGOR'S GONE!

R. Chast

The Museum of Norman L.

First, let's meet the caretakers, Mr. and Mrs. L.

Here is the very spoon with which Norman L. took his first bite of solid food.

You might want to peruse the toys which Norman first played with as a tot.

PUFFY

PLEASE DO NOT LEAN ON GLASS!

SPOON

You are now in one of the most sacred shrines of all: The Room of the Blanket.

"BABA"
No photographs, please.

Mr. and Mrs. L. would be all too pleased to show you some of the garments of the young lad.

Perhaps you are wondering, what about the mind? What was the mind of Norman all about?

Well, why don't you spend a couple of days in the Normanic Archives and find out?

REPORT CARD
1959 - 1975
MATH EXAMS
1961 - 1975
ENGLISH EXAMS

NORMAN'S POETRY
1957 - 1979
BOOK REPORTS
1961 - 1965
BOOK REPORTS

TE
19
TH
19
ILL

Remember, every Tuesday is Movie Night.

But come anytime— the Museum is always open.

THE MUSEUM OF NORMAN
4-N

WELCOME

R. Chast

MORE NONTRADITIONAL FAMILY UNITS

Guy, Chair, Three-Way Lamp

A Woman, Her Daughter, Forty-four My Little Ponies

The Troy Triplets and Their Personal Trainer

Two Guys, Two Gals, Two Phones, a Fax, and a Blender

R. Chast

KIDS' POINT OF VIEW

UNDERSTANDING YOUR PARENTS

{ TABLE OF CONTENTS }

p. Clt

HAIKU by KEVIN

Fourth grade is the pits.
Mrs. Tate is fat and mean,
And I hate her guts.

Jimmy's so lucky.
He gets everything he wants.
I wish I was him.

Mom, Mom, Mom. _Mom_. **MOM!**
Why can't I get my ear pierced?
Why can't I? **Why not?**

MY WEEKLY ENQUIRER

★ ★ ★ THE ONLY TABLOID THAT'S <u>JUST</u> <u>FOR</u> <u>KIDS!</u> ★ ★ ★

RAFFI IS AN ALIEN!

SECRET PHOTO: TAKEN OUT OF COSTUME

MISS PIGGY'S HIDDEN AFFAIR WITH BERT

"WE'LL MARRY IN JUNE," SHE SAYS

LAMB CHOP'S SECRET ADDICTION TO CHILDREN'S TYLENOL

"LITTLE" MERMAID GAINS 75 LBS.; GOES TO FAT FARM IN TUCSON, ARIZONA

ERNIE'S COSMETIC SURGERY BACKFIRES-NOW HE LOOKS LIKE A NINJA TURTLE!

photos page 11 →

R. Cls

CHILDREN OF THE
INNER SUBURB

Brian

Thinks going to the mall is really fun.

Jenny

Often plays outside in the yard unattended.

Zachary

Has never heard the term "PRIVATE HOUSE."

R. Clf

PLAYING THE YOUTH CARD

THE FIRST KIDS CLUB
Yeah, I remember when I was the cat's pajamas! NUMERO UNO! THE ONE AND ONLY!
All I had to do was show a little wear and tear - and KABOOM! Here's comes NUMBER TWO!
I did my best, but I guess it just wasn't enough.
R. Ch

CHILDREN'S HOUSE OF HORRORS

The Hall of Snowsuits

The Plate Where All the Different Foods Are Touching One Another

The Gallery of Inexplicable Fears

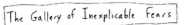

Live Demonstration of The Shampoo (1:00, 3:00, 5:00)

R.Chst

THE LITANY OF FUN

...and then we got on the bus and then we all had treats and then we sang songs and then we played games and then Billy and Kenny got into a fight over a Ninja and then we got off the bus and then we had a snack and then we stood in line and then we got tickets and then we went into the zoo and then we saw the Wild Africa exhibit and then we got back in line and then we saw the Hall of Bats exhibit and then we were talking and laughing and then we got back in line and then Mrs. Hudson got mad at us and then we got quieter and then we marched to the picnic tables and then we sat down and then some of us got hot dogs at the concession stand and then some of us got burgers with cheese and some of us got burgers without cheese and then we ate lunch and then we got back in line and then we went to the Wild World of Monkeys and then we went to Our Undersea Friends and then Mrs. Hudson yelled at us some more and then we had a snack under a tree and then we got back in line and then we went to the souvenir shop and then we bought monkey stickers or erasers that had bat heads or T-shirts that said "I've Been to Herkimer Zoo" or key chains with little whales hanging from them and then we walked back to Parking Lot B and then we got on the bus and then Mr. Jones drove us home and here I am.

R. Chast

THE BOY WITH THE FERAL PARENTS

MYSTERY ILLNESSES
OF CHILDHOOD

REAL · BONA FIDE · NOT FAKED

Three-Hour Virus

This is a genuine bug that lasts for an entire morning. By the time it passes, it's too late to go to school.

Nauseitis

Suddenly, one just feels really, really nauseous for about an hour, usually during math or social studies. If you lie down, it goes away.

Out-of-the-Blue Flu

This one comes up a lot when your folks have an evening out planned. Oh, well! Luckily, it's usually over in a few hours.

One-Day Bug

You just feel horrible. The only cure is to be waited on hand and foot.

Ma? Can you bring me some chocolate milk? And a fig Newton?

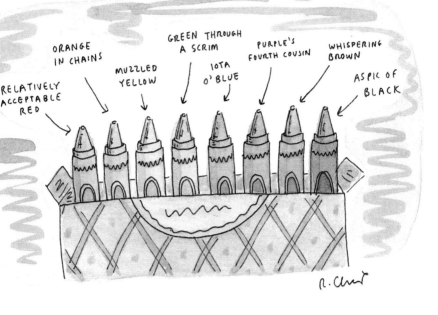

COFFEE TABLE BOOKS
for
KIDS

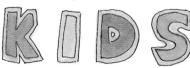

Over two hundred glossy,
full-page color photographs of
the world's best things. Ages 1-10.

They're all in here, from satin-
trimmed cashmere extravaganza to
the rattiest shmatta. Birth - 2 years.

Are they truly concerned for
your "safety"? Can they really
not "afford" it? Or are they just
yanking your chain? You'll
never know. Ages 3-11.

Picture after picture of
adults being caught doing idiotic
things. You'll bust a gut.
Age 2-18.

R. Clv

THE SANTA BELIEF CHART OF TREVOR B.

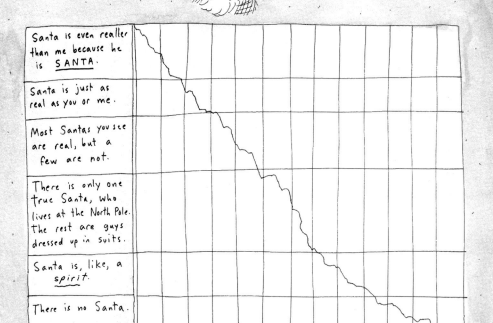

Santa is even realler than me because he is <u>SANTA</u>.													
Santa is just as real as you or me.													
Most Santas you see are real, but a few are not.													
There is only one true Santa, who lives at the North Pole. The rest are guys dressed up in suits.													
Santa is, like, a <u>*spirit*</u>.													
There is no Santa.													

1987 1988 1989 1990 1991 1992 1993 1994 1995 1996 1997 1998 1999 2000

Why One's Parents Got Married

A really convincing guy told them that if they tied the knot they'd get a zillion dollars _and_ learn all the secrets of the cosmos.

Sounds good to me!

Me, too!

An alien civilization threatened to blow up the planet unless the two were wed.

They _were_, in fact, for a brief time, the only man and woman on Earth, except for a nearby justice of the peace.

I do.

I do.

R. Chast

Education

HOMEWORK FOR TOMORROW

Use the words "mung bean" in a sentence.
Do the sevens, eights, and nines tables.
Study for spelling quiz!
Map of South America.
Natural resources diorama.
Write a one-page ess... n Amerigo Vespucci.
Book report due!
Bring in straws.

You have a power job... a power address... a power mate...

BUT...

DO YOU HAVE A

POWER CHILD?

① Child's instrument: ☐ Piano, flute, oboe, violin. ☐ Cymbals.

② Clothing: ☐ One-of-a-kind items from Soho boutiques; Ralph Lauren Kids. ☐ Nine Inch Nails T-shirt, but it's _clean_.

③ Food: ☐ Ethnic, vegetarian, French. ☐ Lucky Charms.

④ School orientation: ☐ Finds $14,000 a year school an agreeable part of his or her journey to society's highest strata. ☐ Recess is in seven minutes, oh boy.

⑤ Friends: ☐ Merit scholars, **chess** champions, molecular biologists, etc. ☐ Let's just say they're _carefree_.

⑥ Friends' parents: ☐ Brilliant, attractive, successful individuals. ☐ Doing their best, considering.

FOR EVALUATION, SEND QUESTIONNAIRE WITH $2.00 TO: Power Child
P.O. Box 92739
New York, New York 10000

Uncelebrated Child Prodigies

Melvin P., Doorman: age 3½

Doreen A., Personal Trainer: age 5

Lon J., Reupholsterer: age 4

R. Chast

HOME SCHOOLING:

COURSE LISTINGS, FALL '93

1 | Math In Our World

Junior and Missy explore ways in which math relates to daily life.

2 | The Wonders of Nature ✳

Junior and Missy go out in the yard to expand their horizons.

3 | Health and Nutrition

Lunchtime provides ample opportunity for Junior and Missy to learn about these important subjects.

4 | Learning About Animation ✳

Junior and Missy watch cartoons for about an hour.

5 | Reading

The joys of the world of print are explored.

6 | History

Junior and Missy sit on the sofa with Mom and look at photographs of what life was like before they were born. CLASS DISMISSED!

✳ = INDEPENDENT STUDY

THE LAST SUPPER

from # PERFECT WORLD.

TOYS & GAMES, INC.

Water Non-Guns

These squirters can shoot a jet of water *fifteen feet* - plus, they're shaped like cruciferous vegetables.

Environmentally Aware Dolls

Your child will have the time of his or her life playing with *Rosie the Recycler.*

Say! You're using too *many* paper towels!

Non-Competitive Board Games

No more screaming and yelling about who won, who lost, or who cheated. Just hours and hours of contented play.

IT'S A TIE!

LET'S NOT KEEP SCORE

Self-Esteem-Building Craft Kits

These kits are impossible for your kid to screw up. Perfect results every time.

r.chs

DAD BUNNY MOM BUNNY BROTHER BUNNY SISTER BUNNY

INTRODUCING...

THE BERNSTEIN BUNNIES

...where somebody is always learning a lesson about something.

THE BERNSTEIN BUNNIES in

TOO MUCH MIXING

Brother Bunny learns why it's not a good idea to drink beer, wine, Mai-Tais, and Crème de Cacao all at the same sitting.

THE BERNSTEIN BUNNIES learn about

GOSSIP

Sister Bunny tells a friend a particularly sensitive bit of news. Forty seconds later, it's all over town.

THE BERNSTEIN BUNNIES do a

REALLY STUPID THING

One day, Dad Bunny was under a lot of pressure. Plus, he was having a mid-life crisis. Find out how he re-ordered his priorities.

THE BERNSTEIN BUNNIES enter

FAMILY COUNSELING

The Bernsteins learn that seeing a **therapist** is nothing to be ashamed of.

r.chast

CITY CAMPS

Camp Ci-Ne-Mah
862 Irving Place

Boys and girls aged five to fifteen spend six
weeks going from movie house to movie house.
Activities include blockbusters, crime dramas,
comedies, serious European films, and revivals.

Camp Shah-Ping
9631 Lexington Avenue

An unforgettable experience for children
aged seven to fourteen. They'll make friends
for life as they browse through New
York's finest department stores and
boutiques. Established 1924.

Camp Res-Toh-Rant
6475 East 89th Street

A wonderful summer lies ahead for campers aged
six to fifteen. They will receive expert instruction
in dealing with various cuisines, and also in
making reservations, tipping, and paying by credit card.

I'd like to put
this on Visa,
please.

Camp In-Dor-O
1839 West End Avenue

Our forty-fifth year in this ten-room prewar
apartment. A noncompetitive atmosphere
for the quieter, less active child. We offer
reading, coloring, TV, chess, Monopoly,
lanyard-making, and more.

r·Chj

BLACK MARKET

CHILDREN'S BOOKS

Sharky

An easy-to-read, brightly illustrated tale of Sharky. the hungry denizen of several East Coast beaches.

Some "Heroes," Huh?

This well-researched text provides youngsters with everything they need to know about **admired athletes, scientists, artists, presidents, etc.** of past and present.

DRUG ADDICT   ALCOHOLIC   WOMANIZER   ALL-AROUND CREEP

Aliens from Pluto vs. Mutant Robots

Another **exciting** story from the author of *Cannibal Ghosts vs. Giant Martian Bees.* Guaranteed to keep even the sleepiest sleepyhead awake all night.

Gee, My Mom and Dad Are Old!

One day Lisa realizes something about her folks.

Hildegarde, The Twerp

Hildegarde is disliked by everybody in her class simply because she is fat and has a stupid name. By the end of the book, matters have only gotten worse.

Yuck!

Please don't make me sit next to her.

Weapons From A To Z

A charming way for children to familiarize themselves with the alphabet. Spans the gamut from axe to zipgun.

Blunt instrument

Cannon

r. Chast

FROM AESOP'S CHILDHOOD NOTEBOOKS

The Lion and The Anteater

A little story about a proud, talented lion and his obtuse, disgusting creative writing teacher.

The Owl and The Hyena

A short yet instructive tale concerning a fable-inventing owl and a cute but silly hyena who thinks that everything is just a BIG, FAT **JOKE**.

Oh, Aesop, you SLAY me! Ha ha ha

The Arabian Steed and The Oxen

A vignette in which a graceful, parable-spinning young Arabian steed proves to the two oxen who live with him that they are not his parents.

Aesop, dinner in 5 minutes.

R. Chast

GUT COURSES
AT MISS MORESBY'S PRESCHOOL

1024 ~ Arts and Crafts

Grab three crayons at random and make a bunch of marks on the paper. Miss Moresby will go bananas.

1168 ~ Puppet Show

All you have to do is sit there and watch Miss Moresby do a Punch and Judy thing. It's a cinch.

2305 ~ Sing-a-Long

Just sing as loud as you can, and you can't go wrong.

2779 ~ Show and Tell

Don't be shy. Just get up there and talk about the lint in your pocket. A guaranteed "A."

ADDITIONS TO
THE RAINBOW CURRICULUM

SARAH HAS TWO MOMMIES WHO ARE BARRY MANILOW FANS

Jason's Daddy Wears a Rug

JENNIFER'S MOM AND DAD VACATION AT A NUDIST COLONY IN THE POCONOS

REBECCA HAS FOUR GRANDMAS AND THEY ALL WORK OUT WITH HEAVY HANDS

MARK'S PARENTS ARE ALIENS

ALL OF LAURA'S MOMS ARE CRUMMY POETS

STEPHEN'S THREE SHRINER UNCLES

NICOLE'S MOMMY AND DADDY BUY THEIR CLOTHES AT SEARS

R. Chast

ACTUAL QUESTIONS ASKED
BY A SEVEN-YEAR-OLD

? ? ? ? ? ?

Is there an oil that is really sour that they give kids?

How much is a zebra worth?

If you shot a bullet, would it go into space?

Are there poisonous cactuses that could kill you if you got pricked?

How many degrees can melt skin?

Are there aliens? Could there be? How many? 25,000?

Are monkeys ever mean? How about small monkeys?

How much do wigs cost? Could they cost $1,000,000?

Is the President still alive?

Is the guy who walked on the Moon rich? Is he richer than us?

Do you have to get special markings to go to China?

If a kid got born with three legs, and his parents wanted to leave the extra leg on, could the doctor force them to let the kid have the leg removed?

TEENS
BOOKS BY THE GALLON
ADOLESCENT ALLEY
FOR ALL YOUR TEEN-AGE NEEDS
BIG MAMA
YES! WE HAVE LAVA LAMPS
THREE'S COMPANY

THE WORLD'S FIRST GENETICALLY ENGINEERED
HUMAN HITS ADOLESCENCE

HIGH SCHOOL DIPLOMAS OF TOMORROW

Attendance Diploma

For those who didn't understand a thing, but were there most of the time.

Nice Guy Diploma

For complete non-learners who were extremely popular with teachers and fellow pupils.

Bare-Bones Diploma

For kids who can read a TV listing, sign their names, and add up what's in their wallet.

Good Faith Diploma

For students who never went to class, but you sense that if they did, would have excelled academically.

childhood's end

REVISIONIST HISTORY

THE LAST OF THE
PUNITIVE DAMAGES

Never bought daughter Barbie:
$ 3,000,000

Bought daughter Barbie, but it was the wrong one:
$ 4,000,000

Bought the right Barbie, but denied daughter Midge, Ken, or Skipper:
$ 6,000,000

Bought too much Barbie stuff for daughter, causing psychic harm:
$ 12,000,000

THE COMPLETE CYCLE

THE WAGES OF SIN

R. Chast

JUST DO IT

MIDDLE AGE

JUNE '97

THE MAGAZINE FOR YOU - YEAH, YOU!

See That Old Lady Sitting Across From You? That's How You Look, Too.

"I Was the Oldest Person at the Dead Concert": A SPECIAL REPORT

So You've Turned Into Your Dad.

R. Chast

THE FALLINGS-IN-LOVE OF
DEBBIE DEBISTON

Mom

This toy

Miss Tilden, of Miss Tilden's Silly Schoolhouse, channel 3

These shoes

Stanley and Jester

Carolyn Crane (her sycophants)

These shoes

Kenny Axton

Paul McCartney
MEET THE BEATLES
Hi, Debbie!

Hippies
FLOWER
PEACE

Phil Ochs

Fred Tannenbaum and his entire family
WOODSTOCK
MAKE LOVE

These shoes

The theatre

Hamlet
...

Andrew Tipton

Japanese food

Majolica

These shoes

Buster

r.chr